Sister M---
You and ---
for your supp---
pray God's choice
blessings upon your life.
Be inspired as you
journey through
"Bound To Be Free"
Marva J. Edwards
2011

Bound To Be Free
Breaking Free from Domestic Violence

Marva J. Edwards

AuthorHouse™
1663 Liberty Drive
Bloomington, IN 47403
www.authorhouse.com
Phone: 1-800-839-8640

© *2010 Marva J. Edwards. All rights reserved.*

No part of this book may be reproduced, stored in a retrieval system, or transmitted by any means without the written permission of the author.

First published by AuthorHouse 5/26/2010

ISBN: 978-1-4490-8514-8 (e)
ISBN: 978-1-4490-8513-1 (sc)
ISBN: 978-1-4490-8517-9 (hc)

Library of Congress Control Number: 2010901828

Printed in the United States of America
Bloomington, Indiana

This book is printed on acid-free paper.

Bound to Be Free is dedicated to:

First, to my mother, the late Barbara Malone Johnson, who was a domestic violence survivor and one who provided safety and support for some who suffered the same.

MY MOTHER WHEN I WAS A TEENAGER

To my great-grandmother, the late Daisy Bell Cornelius; my grandmother, the late Virginia Malone; and my great-aunt, Maebelle Smoot.

*MY GREAT GRANDMOTHER (MY MOTHER'S MOTHER)
DAISY BELL CORNELIUS*

I also dedicate this book to every man and to every woman who has suffered domestic violence to any degree and to every man, woman, boy, and girl whose life has been affected. To the memory of those whose lives have been lost as a result of domestic violence, especially to those police officers who were sworn to serve and to protect and lost their lives doing so!

I salute each of you, and I share in the experience of the pain and the devastation, and prayerfully the hope that abides with you as well, that your experience has brought to you and to those you love.

Contents

Acknowledgments xi

Introduction xiii

    Chapter 1. Where Am I? 1

    Chapter 2. Running Scared 5

    Chapter 3. Remembering the Red Flags 9

    Chapter 4. True Colors 19

    Chapter 5. Covered Wounds 27

    Chapter 6. Bracing for Battle 31

    Chapter 7. Making Another Exit! 35

    Chapter 8. Taking a Stand 41

    Chapter 9. A Collective View 53

    Chapter 10. Hurt People Hurt People! 67

    Chapter 11. The Power of Abuse! 71

    Chapter 12. Bound to Be Free 79

    Chapter 13. Generational Curses 93

    Chapter 14. Characteristics of Abusers 105

Acknowledgments

To God be all the glory for what has and for what is to come. Thank God for bringing me to a healthy place and for helping this endeavor become a reality.

While bringing *Bound to Be Free* together, I had to call upon many people to make this possible. You all have supported me in ways that have encouraged me more than you know.

My deepest appreciation and thanks go to my loving husband, Robert, for being my biggest supporter, sounding board, and initial editor. To my children, Khatara, KieSharra, Kadeem, and Kalio, who have allowed me to share a part of their lives here as well, and have contributed to my work.

Thanks to my other family members and to my dear friends who have cheered me on and who have believed in me through this process of completion.

Thanks to every man and woman of God who spoke life into my very spirit that encouraged me to look up and to live!

With humbleness of heart, a very special thank you to my late bishop, Johnny H. Covington, who taught me to walk by faith and to believe in God for anything.

Special thanks to the family and children services of the Piedmont, Greensboro, North Carolina, who assisted me in obtaining the assistance that I needed in a time of crisis years ago along with Alyce Bitticks. Special thanks also to Bishop Bernard Wright, who contributed his time and secured the house that my children and I lived in by making it more difficult to be broken into.

God bless each of you immensely!

Introduction

Bound to Be Free is a portion of my life's story and tells of my personal struggles with domestic violence. It portrays real-life events I encountered in a relationship and in a marriage that was bound for destruction. In many situations, I failed to recognize the red flags—an error in judgment that would later cost me dearly. I went from asking myself, *Where am I?* to wondering, *Who am I?* While depicting the power of prayer and perseverance, with a hope and trust in a loving Father who wills goodness for his children, this book also demonstrates a level of fear of man but yet a level of faith in God. *Bound to Be Free* exposes the evil and control of abuse, whether it is by a male or a female, with constant cries for help in what seemed to be a hopeless and dark situation. Here you will find that domestic violence doesn't discriminate; it knows no gender, no age limit, and no religion. It is vile, and it is also evil. The power of abuse can carry from one generation to another, as is shared here, but it can also manifest in so many different forms, and to so many different people connected to the abuser. *Bound to Be Free* shares the will to believe that God will do what only he can. It is meant to give courage and hope to every reader. It shows a desire to be free and to live free from abuse, and for the abuser the courage to be free and live free from abusing. Experience the determination to be free and to take courage to go after that freedom, while having to look evil in the face and make a conscious decision to take a stand and to cease running. Be encouraged, be empowered, and be informed as you take a journey with me into *Bound to Be Free*!

Chapter 1

Where Am I?

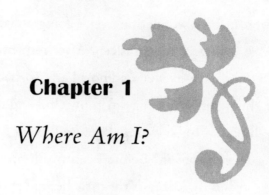

In the midst of another argument over something so trivial, fear has gripped me once again. Suddenly I am hit in the face with such force that it spun me around (something I've only seen in the movies). I spun in what seemed to be extreme slow motion. I feel my body gradually falling to the floor, but I don't have the ability to stop myself from falling.

I have no idea how much time has passed, when I open my eyes. Where am I? It seems that I am somewhere other than at home, as my surroundings are unfamiliar to me. I'm panicked; I'm wondering where my children are. *Does my mother know where I am? What is my telephone number? How did I get here in this bed?* Feeling myself to be in a major state of confusion as to my immediate circumstances, I also feel incredible pain in my face; my head is throbbing intensely. I now realize that I am in a new place—we had just moved some days ago. I cannot say how long to be exact.

I'm extremely thirsty; needing a drink of water, I go into the kitchen to cure my thirst. On the way back from the kitchen, I peep in on my children, as I am wondering what's going on with them. Thank God they are each very much asleep. After returning to my bedroom, I began to drink the water, and now I am worried. As I drink from the glass, the water is running down my chin and my neck. I realize that something has to be wrong, because I never felt it leave my mouth. What does this mean? Before I can finish processing that, thought, I look up and there stands the preacher in the doorway. He's looking at me as though some small disagreement has occurred. He asked me, "Are you all right, honey?" Imagine that I almost hated him in that moment. I certainly did not like him; loving him as a wife was long gone. There was a struggle to love him even as a Christian. He's beaten me in my face and has hit me so hard in my head that I passed out. Yet he has the audacity to ask if I am all right. I never responded to him; his question was not worthy of a response. Surprisingly, he leaves me alone.

I am afraid, lonely, and greatly troubled, but who will hear my plea? Who will even help me? After all, I'm a preacher's wife. Sadly, it's not getting any better—it worsens with every single fight! I must find a way to get out of this living hell I am in!

Lord Jesus, help me. Please help me! I know that my children are not in a safe place; I also know that it is my responsibility to make them safe.

I have to figure out how I will explain a busted lip, a swollen face, and even the constant pain in my head. How will I explain this to my church family, and to my natural family? What in the world will my children think when they look into their mother's face? How will I keep the tears from streaming down my face? Surely my heart will ache when I look into their eyes, knowing that they see my physical pain. Lord God, please help me to leave this place. It's not a home at all!

At some point, my babysitter called my mother and told her what had happened. I know this because one day out of the blue, my mother and one of my sisters showed up at my house. The preacher was outside doing something to his car. I heard screaming and yelling. I ran to the front door, and to my surprise my mother and my sister were giving him a beating, and my mother dared him to touch her! She was yelling and telling him off in her own way! Mind you, he didn't do a thing. I just watched. A part of me was happy, and a part of me was sorrowful.

Chapter 2

Running Scared

As I am preparing for tonight's church service, I have such expectancy for the move of God. I don't care how God shows up; I just need for him to show up for me. I'm extremely excited! I just believe God will help me where I am.

We arrived in Sanford a bit early for the service. The Prophet (the pastor of the church) has invited the preacher and me to come up to his office with him and his wife. We have a cold drink, and they have some conversation with each other. I continue to sit quietly. I have such an unsettling within myself. We all eventually go down to the sanctuary. Praise and worship were going on, and the music was wonderful. It was filled with God's anointing. The word of God was a blessing, and at the end the Prophet ministered to me. He said that the Lord told him that he had anointed me for ministry and that not everyone would be able to walk with me in ministry because of my life's struggles. He also told me that God was going to bless my hands to get wealth because he could trust me. I had mixed emotions—happy and afraid at the same time. Ministry and money? This means incredible challenges in many ways. What a great responsibility. I prayed that God will keep me humble.

We arrive back at the house from Sanford, and the hour is quite late. Our sitter and her husband have decided to stay for the night. The children are all asleep and in their beds.

Morning has come, and the drama has begun already. The preacher comes to me for money. The church he pastors cannot afford to pay him a salary. He does not have other employment, but depends on me. He expects to live off my children's child support, money that I make for doing hair on the side, and food stamps. Because I refuse to comply with his request to give him money and I question him about why he wants it, an argument breaks out. This leads to a physical fight with him despite my fear. Shortly thereafter I am running scared, in my nightgown and a pair of footies, and with the hammer in my hand—which I was somehow able to take from him before he was able to hit me with it. Thank God! I know that it was the grace of God that allowed me to take the hammer from him. Breath is seemingly not in my body, as I am gasping. I'm trying to run as fast as I can, yet it seems as though I am running in slow motion. It seems as though I can't get away fast enough, but I am too afraid to look back. I know it was only the grace of God that allowed me to get that hammer from him! Finally I've made it to Bessemer Avenue;

this is only about a hundred yards away from the house. Yet it seemed to be so much farther. I have no thought for what I am wearing; I am just running scared. Oh, God, please help me. Don't let him catch me. I cannot look behind me. I make it to the Laundromat and store—this was about a mile or so. Thanks be to God, I see a sister from my home church. She sees me as well and allows me to get into her car and regroup. There's no sign of the preacher anywhere in sight. I am so relieved for the moment. However, I have to go back home at some point. This causes me to return with a greater sense of fear. I know that sooner or later when I least expect it, I will have to pay for this. I would have to pay for causing his violent behavior to be exposed and for allowing other people to know what goes on in his house, he would say.

I arrive at home scared as ever but trying to present a strong front. I never wanted him to know how afraid I really was. My children were at home waiting with the sitter. I'm sure they were wondering where I was and what was going on. They were still asleep when I got of the bed earlier while all of the arguing was going on. The sitter was very reluctant to leave me at home with the preacher. She needed to go home, so I told her not to worry about it. Little did I know that at some point she had told my mother about the fight; my mother in turn told my cousin and my brother. I'm afraid here, not knowing what to do or how to behave. I hope to avoid another confrontation, at least for today. It's becoming harder and harder to be successful at that. I feel as though I have a huge wound inside of me growing bigger and bigger all the time. I am starting to feel as though I'm losing my mind. I consider myself to be a strong person, but this is where I am. How can I protect the ministry and preserve the people? I really need someone that I can talk to—someone that I can really open up to. I have a friend, and I feel that I can trust her. My concern is her relationship with the preacher's brother. I am in a bad situation, though; I must take a chance and trust her. I have to trust someone to help me get me and my children through this, even if it is just in being helped to properly process my thoughts. I must get some help. I'm praying and talking with the Lord; I need some direction. I have even turned my plate down! I believe in God for deliverance and for the courage to leave. I am bound with fear, but I must be free. This isn't how it is supposed to be. Here I am a Christian woman, a pastor's wife; this cannot be for real. Scripture declares according to Ephesians 5:25, Husbands, love your wives, even as Christ also loved the church, and gave himself for it; "; this isn't the kind of love I get from the preacher. He seems to be filled with rage; we know that rage certainly doesn't come from God! It's really a time for me to pray like never before. Time for me to pray with all diligence and make my request known unto God. Of course he knows what I have need of even before I ask. It is my place to ask for what I need. I pray for the Lord's protection and for peace within myself that I may get through this.

Chapter 3

Remembering the Red Flags

You know, as the old saying or proverb goes, hindsight is 20/20. I realize now, and I have known for some time that there were many red flags along the way. I have to say that either I overlooked them or I was too naïve to pay attention to them. It is so important that we pay attention to things along the way. We must remember that everything is a sign of something else. There is an old proverb that says what you see is what you get. What you see is oftentimes worse than what you get; that was certainly so in my case. Pay attention to the red flags in your life!

Some years ago when I met the preacher, he was charming and well-spoken, and he chose his words carefully. He was quite attentive. He knew what to say and also when to say it. The preacher sounded like one would expect a preacher to sound; he was well-dressed and presented himself as a gentleman. Red flag

I remember that on the first date I had with him, he stopped at the automatic teller machine off Summit Avenue. We were going to Libby Hill Seafood restaurant. We were right at the restaurant; however, he wanted to go the one on the other side of town. Red flag.

As we talked over dinner, I inquired about the church where he was the pastor and its location. He responded by telling me that it was in Siler City; however, he would be relocating to Greensboro as soon as he could. I cannot remember at this time his reasoning for making the transition. The preacher was often in Greensboro on Sunday mornings instead of in Siler City. I wondered why he was not ministering to his own congregation each Sunday. He had not invited me to attend worship services with him either. Red flags.

Months have gone by now, and I've fallen in my walk with God. I've become so self-engaged with my own loneliness, that I have allowed myself to become sexually involved with the preacher. I'm pregnant and feeling such enormous guilt. It wouldn't be too much to say that I'm devastated! Here I am having put myself in a situation of having another child without having been married—not even in a stable relationship. The preacher is spreading the news with such joy, and I'm still trying to forgive myself for having fallen from my place in God. Red flags.

Over a period of time—I'm not sure how long; maybe a couple of months had passed by—things seemed to have been getting better. Then I discovered that the car the preacher had been driving and leading me to believe was his, really wasn't. The car belonged to a deacon of his church. Since this discovery, he now has to transport the deacon to work and wherever it is he needs to go, and then return him to his said destination. Red flags.

Several weeks have gone by, and the preacher is now parking the car in what I call very strange places. He's parking up the street around the corner and sometimes in another parking lot in the complex. He justifies this by saying he doesn't want people all in his business. He states that he needs privacy just as everyone else does. He sounds so convincing. Red flags.

By now the deacon has been looking for the preacher in hopes of having his car returned. I realize this is in part why the preacher has been parking the car in strange places. So the preacher has been evading him all of this time. He would park at another unit where the parking was in the back of the unit and sometimes even around the corner. I can no longer deal with the constant lying, for the lies are more than I can number or even remember. We break up because of the constant arguing, lies, and my lack of trust in him. After the breakup, he says to me, "If I can't be with you, then I have nothing left to live for." Red flags.

He continued to talk of committing suicide. This made me feel a great sense of responsibility for trying to help him; I feel that I must find some way to help him. I'm feeling stuck! I'm in and out of this relationship; it's off and on again and again. I'm feeling guilty because of the preacher's depression and his talking of committing suicide each time he thinks I may break up with him. The thought of the preacher taking his life because of me is a burden I don't wish to live with. It's difficult to stay away from him. He seems to be so involved in my life. I'm feeling overwhelmed. The preacher calls all the time from morning until night. Then at other times, he just shows up with no warning. Red flags.

I'm sinking and getting farther and farther away from God. My neighbor who is also my friend has become a much-needed support for me. As I talk more freely with my neighbor, he tells me, "This guy is crazy. Are you sure he's a preacher? Something is wrong with him."

Today is the Fourth of July. My eldest brother and his girlfriend have decided to take my two girls with them to see the fireworks after the Fun Fourth festivities are over. My son and I return home, and it is late. At about 11:00 PM, my doorbell rang. I'm startled because of the lateness of the hour. I go to the window and ask who's at the door. It happens to be the preacher's sister. What could she possibly want this time of night?! She said, "Girl, I need to talk to you. It's an emergency!" I open the door, and she suddenly announces that she has to go lock her car door. I must say I was quite concerned, because this girl usually doesn't even talk to me. We don't even have that type of relationship for her to be coming to my apartment. I assume she went on to her car, but when she returned she had another female with her. She looked somewhat familiar to me. She was tall and very stocky—what my mother would call a country build. They sit down and began to snicker. At this point I know something is wrong. I'm just over five months pregnant, and this situation is making me quite nervous. I'm sitting on the sofa, and they are sitting on the love seat. They appear to be high. My son has gotten up out of bed, so I go to get him back down. As I sit back down, the other female asks me why I have been cheating on her cousin.

I responded by saying, "I'm not cheating on anyone because I don't have anyone, and who am I supposed to be cheating with?"

She named the guy she was talking about and said, "That's who." Just then I knew that she was about to get up. As I began to get up, she rushed toward me from across the room. She hit me in the face, and I fell over on the end table. I thought I needed something to help me defend and protect myself. I went into the kitchen, remembering quickly that I don't even keep very sharp knives in the kitchen because of the children. I grabbed the hammer out of the drawer and ran back into the living room. They were still there (it must have been the drugs they were on). As they saw me coming with the hammer in my hand, the preacher's sister got up first to escape through the front door, and the other female, who had hit me, was following quickly behind her. The other female fell as she was going out, and I hit her in the back with the hammer. I raised the hammer again, with the thought of busting her head wide open. I could have easily hit her again, because she was moving slowly. I was angry and in survival mode, but I could not allow myself to hurt her in that way, despite what had been done to me. I just held the hammer in the air as she looked straight into my eyes. God's mercy was with both of us, and to him be the glory. She got up and ran around the back side of the apartment.

As I went back into the house, I noticed that I had blood on my shirt, and I hurried into the bathroom. When I looked into the mirror, I saw how bloody my mouth was. My lips and the side of my face were swollen. I felt so violated and mad, to say the least. I chose not to call any of my family; I just didn't know how to handle what had just happened. I later figured out who the other female was. She liked my neighbor and was at his house a few times when I went to use his phone. I wanted to have both of them thrown in jail! Even though the preacher's sister never hit me, I held her just as responsible because she brought the other female to my apartment. When I went downtown to take out a warrant, I found out that I needed a current address to complete the warrant. (Eventually I obtained an address, but the warrant was never served.)

It's about three or four in the morning on the next day, and I am having major abdominal pains; my stomach is really tightening up. To the emergency room I go, and the doctor said that because of the incident, the baby was under stress. He said that rest would help to normalize things in most cases. I'm trying to process the whole situation: how and why would the aunt of my unborn child bring someone, twice my size, to do me bodily harm and endanger the unborn baby's well-being? Red flags.

I remember the preacher calling the next day, saying how shocked he was about what had happened. Oh, he was so mad about what had happened. "Just wait. I'm going to tell my sister a thing or two …" The preacher used this situation to start calling more frequently. He begins to talk as though he's focused and ready to do as a man should—without gainful employment, though. Imagine that! Red flag.

On September 12, 1991, I go into labor. At seven and one-half months, my baby is born. He is early; he is a little jaundiced, but other than that he is healthy. Thanks be to God! The preacher arrives after the baby is born, and he has a few other people with him, none of whom I am acquainted with. This is a joyous occasion: I'm happy at the birth of my son and also relieved that it is over. The preacher is proud of his new son and begins to share how much he wants to be a family. He proclaims that he has changed and states that the Lord has been dealing with him about things. He shows himself to be quite attentive; his visits with the baby became more and more frequent. I really wanted to believe him. I must say that I allowed him to persuade me. We consequently resumed a relationship, and as time goes by, I allow him to stay over some nights. Red flags!

The preacher and I were talking one day, and he began to share more in detail how he was abused and mistreated as a child. He also spoke of how poor his family relationships were and said that he had a daughter that he could not see, because he and the mother didn't see eye to eye on how to rear her. The preacher had my attention and my sympathy. I truly felt sorry for him and could not understand how his own could treat him this way. Red flags!

I've finally gotten to a place where I am more committed in my walk with God! I'm striving to live a holy life and to walk upright before him. I'm spending more time in prayer and trying to work on me! I feel something I haven't felt in a very long time—that is, encouraged. It has been a long time coming. While I desire more quiet time for my children and for myself, it is increasingly difficult. I face the daily challenge of getting them to quiet down for a nap and at bedtime as well. Most of my neighbors are young college students away from home. The norm for them is parties, loud music, and late nights filled with noise and company. I now have to be more concerned when my children go out to play. I really hope to move soon. The preacher is trying to encourage me to move out into the country, somewhere near Brown Summit. I have heard of the area, but I have no idea as to where it is. Needless to say, I am not the least bit interested. I don't even have a driver's license. In this he was trying to get me to move to a more isolated location where I would not know anyone. Red flag!

Eventually we do move, as I have found a house not too far from our previous residence. My children have their own private yard where they can run freely, happily, and without my having to worry about strange people trafficking through, or up and down the walk. One day while we were out riding, the preacher noticed a building nearby, and after checking further he learned that it was for rent. I must say he was filled with excitement. He goes through the logistics of speaking with the owner and is able to secure the building (for ministry) with some type of agreement. He still has no job, but he was able to manipulate his way. He begins to clean it up immediately and has service on the following Sunday. I have no idea as to how the utilities were handled, but they were all on except for the heat. Following this, he starts talking about getting married, something I've always wanted for myself. I just wasn't sure. After talking and listening to a few others, I agreed, but I think it was much too quickly. A week later we married. No wedding, no family, just a ceremony in my house. I'm married now, every girl's dream. Yeah, right!

Chapter 4

True Colors

The ministry seems to have been going okay for several months. The assistant pastor and his wife and children are very faithful to the work of the ministry. However, the assistant pastor's wife seems to be taking an unusual interest in the preacher! She and the preacher seem to have quite a bit to talk and laugh about. I notice her being eager to serve him, and he is happy to make his requests known. I'm really feeling uncomfortable about the whole thing. She makes it a point to look my way whenever she does something to see if I'm looking, and then she gives me what I perceive to be a sneaky grin. Initially she was very pleasant, but that was short-lived, and now she is rather sharp and short with me. She prepares food items for the preacher only, rather than for his family. I wouldn't trust her food enough for me or for my children to eat it anyway. She looks with a smile, yet her eyes have a devious look.

The preacher's true colors are starting to shine through once again. He has become quite verbally abusive, and this has also led to his hitting me again! I feel weak and unable to defend myself against him and such violent behavior. Actually, I'm afraid of him. He has also begun to show his anger with some of the church members, so what else can I expect? We've only been married for such a short period of time, and already I regret having ever gotten myself into this mess. Arguments are steadily increasing, and so have the physical fights. I remember the fight we had after the one where I had taken the hammer from him and ran. After this fight I insisted that he leave, and he actually left the house, to my surprise, and began living in the church. He came by later the next night, looking cold and pitiful. There was no heat on at the church, and he wanted some food and something hot to drink. I find it to be interesting how someone so abusive and controlling can become so pitiful. Of course I felt sorry for him, and I thought God would not be happy with me for allowing him to live this way.

The evangelist (assistant pastor's wife) found it needful to take care of the preacher during the time he was living at the church. The assistant pastor had become quite suspicious of the wife and the preacher's relationship. He told me himself, and I felt likewise. One day in particular she went to take the preacher some lunch. Her husband waited for some time and finally went to the church. When he arrived, he had to knock on the door because he had allowed his wife to use his key to the church. After he had been knocking and calling out for a few minutes, according to the assistant pastor, his wife finally came to the door. Her clothing was not as it had been when she left home. The preacher came out, and his hair was as though he had just gotten out of bed, and his pants were unzipped. He said, "The preacher had a caught-in-the-act, pitiful game-face look!" Of course, they both declared their innocence. Once again his true colors are shining through. Anything that's still on the inside will come out after a while.

I suppose as time went by, the wounds of the assistant pastor were healed, or he loved his wife enough to accept her relationship with the preacher. Or he allowed himself to go into a state of denial. Either way, he began to allow the preacher to use his wife's car and later allowed him to drop his wife off at work and then use her car. I could not believe for a moment that all of this was going on; I was angered by it as well. I had absolutely no say in the decisions that the preacher was making, unless it was to his total benefit. At times I wished she would just go elsewhere, but that was just wishful thinking!

Eventually, due to all of the circumstances and suspicions surrounding the preacher and the evangelist, and also the lack of trust and honesty, the assistant pastor leaves his wife (the evangelist). I must say he was very hurt and disappointed, because he thought of the preacher as a leader and a trustworthy man of God! With his wife, the trust was broken, and I guess it was more than he was able or willing to work through. May the Lord have mercy! The preacher is still using the car, and they are in each other's presence more and more. When I say something, he accuses me of being jealous and says I must think he wants her. The truth was that he did want her, and was having her, but wasn't man enough to say so. The truth would not have mattered at this point, because I already knew what the truth was! Their relationship was obviously more than what they were admitting, and it was at the least more than what was appropriate. Also by now, I realize that she is definitely not the only woman he is working on being with, if he hasn't been with someone else already.

My brother came into town today, although I haven't seen him yet. I later spoke with him on the phone. He told me that he and my cousin were coming over to talk with the preacher. He told me he did not want me to be at home when they spoke. I have no recollection as to where I went; however, I do know that when I returned home the preacher was crying and said that my brother and my cousin had "jumped on him."

The preacher asked me why I had them to do that, and I responded by saying, "I thought they just wanted to talk to you."

Sometimes I feel that I am praying ineffectively. I'm not hearing from God in regard to some directions, and at this time I need him as I never have before. I seem to be at a standstill, and for me this is a scary place to be, given all of the dynamics of what has been going on. I have less and less trust for the evangelist; I know she prays against me and even encourages others to work against me. Just think, a few months ago, I really thought the evangelist was a respectable and mature Christian. How wrong I was. Change is needed for me, and change is needed within me.

As I was taking the kids for a walk one day, I notice a group of men working on a house nearby. I asked the contractor if he had other houses. He said he might have one available soon. He took us to look at it, and I loved it right away. To God be the glory. I received a letter in the mail from the housing authority just about a week later, saying I had an orientation for Section 8. I attended the orientation and received my certificate for a three-bedroom house. I was so thankful to God! The house was ready within a couple of weeks, and we moved in. Talk about being happy—that was an incredible happy moment. The house was very nice, spacious, and well kept, to say the very least. The yard is very large and fenced in. This is a great thing. I was praying and believing in God for change, and for this change I rejoice. Let me make it clear: that moment of happiness was short-lived, as the preacher becomes more unveiled. The lies and the deception take on a new face altogether. He lies about going to work at a second-shift job that I learn doesn't exist. The company he keeps is most questionable. He now spends a lot of time in Burlington, where the evangelist has moved. He actually goes there to pick her up to attend church in Greensboro. Oh, by the way, she has been appointed his assistant pastor; what a joke! This is so crazy! The saga continues, with his accusing me of being used by the devil when I question his whereabouts. He tells me that he is the head and I need to learn my place as a wife. He is more aggressive and full of threats.

I'm under constant stress and wonder what the next moment holds for me. Getting married wasn't the right thing for me to do; things are not any better since our marriage, but rather worse. Have you ever wondered how you ended up in a certain situation? That's where I am. How did my life become this!

There's a homeless shelter around the corner from my house. I decided to go over and to make myself known. I wanted to see if I could start having Bible study with the women and the children there. I wanted some opportunity to minister to women that were hurting. The director there allowed me to come over once a week, but at other times I just walked through and spoke to everyone. Sometimes I went there because I was looking for some consolation for myself; however, I think I also wanted to see how the women there were starting their lives over. My time spent there was only about six months. This is when the Lord let me know that I needed to be healed before ministering on that level. I must admit, I realized that I was ministering out of my own hurt, my need for healing, and my cry for help! Actually, at times I wished I was there at the shelter myself, because it had to be much better than the way that I was living. Although I was in a nice house, it was not a home. There was the appearance of love abiding there, but that was far from the truth. This was such a terrible way to live. This isn't what anyone should call living life, but a living hell instead from one day to the next. Not going to the shelter definitely required some adjusting for me; nevertheless, it was for my good. This move helped me to see how weak and broken my spirit really was. This experience certainly caused me to take a deeper look into my own life circumstances. Let me be clear in saying that the preacher seemed to be happy when I stopped going to the shelter. This was one place for me where he had no control and could not be glorified for the efforts that went on there. You see, he always wanted credit for something others were doing if they were connected to his ministry in any way at all.

Chapter 5

Covered Wounds

I've suffered being assaulted so many times at this point by the preacher, that I've become a pro at covering my wounds and my bruises. The bruises on my neck and my chest were hidden beneath a full-necked blouse or a turtleneck, and the other scratches on my body were covered easily because of my modest style of dressing. While I am able to cover the wounds, bruises, and scratches, I am not able to hide the soreness and the pain that I carry in my body from being beaten. When questioned, I simply say that I'm tired or that I don't feel very well.

With this being what my life is like on a regular basis, I learned to smile with the saints even with all of the soreness and pain I felt in my body from the fighting. I even served the preacher his drink in the house of God on many occasions, and with a smile. Certainly not a smile that was sincere, although I don't think others knew. But of course he did. This is what I was expected to do, and out of fear of what I would be confronted with when we arrived back home, I complied. I presented myself as though everything was just fine. There were some Sundays that I went to church with my lip busted and made up some fantastic lie about what had happened. On the inside I'm saying, "Your wonderful bishop (as the preacher calls himself) hit me—that's what happened to me!" I really want to tell some respected person in the ministry, but I'm so afraid at this point. How long will this go on before someone realizes what is really happening here? Will I find someone willing to help me get out of this mess that I've gotten myself into? What can I do here? How long can I play the happy, submissive first lady, honoring her husband (in word only)? This was a cover for the people not to see the truth. My honor for him was nonexistent; however, my wounds were real from the inside out. You know, in the midst of all of these things happening, the preacher presents himself in the public eye to be the loving and caring husband and father.

He seems to have somewhat of the Dr. Jekyll and Mr. Hyde personality. He was sweet one minute, and then he would go off yelling so harshly at the children the next. For some reason, he would be harder on the youngest, the only one that was his by birth. He was only a toddler at the time, but if I would pick him up too quickly, the preacher would have a major fit and demand that I put him down, saying he needed to learn a lesson. The preacher would be offended if he thought for one minute I was trying to rescue my children. It did not matter, though; I could somewhat help myself, but they were helpless and totally innocent. I dealt with whatever I had to, because abusing me was one thing, but mistreating the children was something altogether different.

Three of my children are very tense in the preacher's presence; this is out of fear, not out of obedience or a reverence for him. My eldest is not nearly as afraid of him. My youngest daughter is very timid and would rather not be around him at all; the yelling was enough for her and oftentimes caused her to cry. My eldest daughter and my eldest son seem to be the ones he bothers the least. I always wondered why. I later learned that my oldest daughter's father had threatened him if he ever laid a finger on her. My oldest son's father had pretty much told my son to let him know if the preacher ever bothered him. I have to believe the preacher was also intimidated by him, because he never really bothered my eldest son.

The preacher can be so mean-spirited, and he wills to control those around him. He wants you to speak his language and to dance to his tune. I recall going to a Bojangles in Raleigh one night after a church service. This was just up the street from where we were and not very far at all from the interstate. He felt that I should wait and not spend the money getting something to eat. Mind you, this was my money and not his! Others were hungry as well, but no one else spoke up. He has no employment and hasn't for so long. He went off on me so severely, I had to get out of the car; and mind you, we were in the drive-through line. I didn't think there was enough air in the car for both of us to breathe; clearly I was filled with rage toward him. The preacher not only embarrassed me, but he humiliated me in front of others as though I were nothing. I felt so small; I wished to be able to just walk home for the opportunity to be alone. He got out of the car behind me, cursed me out, and then asked what in hell I was crying for! I have had many people mistreat me in my life. This man I wished evil on this night. I knew it was wrong, and I wanted to justify my feelings to God. I had to come to a place of repentance and keep my guard up!

On the following day, I stated to him how I thought he was wrong in how he treated me, especially in the presence of other people. Oh, no, he couldn't possibly be wrong. I was wrong and not submissive. I remember being so upset that I took a cab over to a friend's house. I was crying uncontrollably. I was clearly in a very bad way. I knew I needed to leave him, but I didn't know how. An evangelist friend of mine noticed bruises and scratches and asked me about them. At this time I shared with her the hell I was living in. Of course she was shocked, not the Bishop was the expression on her face, but then there were some questionable areas of his life, she stated. She knew something was not right about him. I continued to cover my wounds both inside and out with most people. My hope and prayer as always is for God to make a way, as I belong to him!

Chapter 6

Bracing for Battle

There are many things in life that we brace for. We brace for the need to stop suddenly or for a rough ride, we brace for bad news, we brace for a bad storm, and we even brace for an attack or a battle that we see coming ahead. I found myself needing to brace for battle in each of these situations. The preacher's presence meant that a battle had to be fought spiritually and sometimes naturally. Things have gotten to be so bad that I began to sleep in my clothing. Intimacy is long gone. I no longer care for him or even trust him in that way. I must sleep in clothes also, because I never know when I may have to defend myself. Given the fact that I no longer share my body with him, this increases the likelihood of a physical altercation. The preacher has no discretion, in my opinion, at this point. He keeps very late hours and odd company, I'll say. He seemed to like catching me off guard, so he would come in at two or three in the morning maybe, if at all. This particular night when he came in miserably late, he insisted that I wake up because he wanted to talk. It did not matter how late it was or that I was asleep. You see, as always, it was about him. I was certain that he was high on something; this was not the first time this had happened, but this time I was not as afraid as I had been in times past. Prayer and the word of God were working in me. I was determined to be ready, and if I became afraid, I wasn't going to let him know it. When I decided to get up, it wasn't because I was complying with his demand, but because I didn't want to be caught in a defenseless position should I need to defend myself. I have no idea as to what type of expression I had on my face; obviously he didn't like it. He told me I had better get that smirk off my face! I told him he couldn't tell me how to look or something to that effect. He lunged toward me and put his hands around my neck and began to choke me. My body was against the wall. I started to scratch and kick him, and he began to threaten me with what he would do. When he realized that I had scratched him, Lord have mercy! He was most furious, and I was really in a battle. When the fight was over, the children were up and he was leaving. As best as I can recall, I had dialed 911 and left the phone lying down. The police arrived, and he was taken off to jail. I later noticed a small brown bottle on the dresser. I'd never seen that bottle before. I picked it up. I knew it wasn't oil, because after turning it up and down I saw that the liquid in it was too thin. I opened it and smelled it. My nose felt like it had gone through my head with the rest of my body. I felt like he was using some type of drug. Clearly this was a drug. I have no idea as to where he could have gotten it. To my disappointment, the preacher was out of jail the very next day. He was at the door knocking, but I refused to let him in; the kids were running through the house yelling that he was at the door. He eventually called the police on me. They told me I had to let him in because he lived there. Can you believe it?! He appeared to have settled down.

He claims to be looking for a job and wants to go downtown to put in an application with some health-care agency. This was in the Dorothy Bardolph Building. I don't remember, but somehow I knew that there was a place inside where I could go and get help with a 50B, a restraining order of protection. I wanted to go inside so bad while he was gone, but I am so paralyzed with fear of him catching me that I can't move out of the car. My mind takes me outside of the car and into the building, but my body will not follow. I keep telling myself to go ahead, but I can't, because I'm bound by fear. Finally, when he comes out we get into some conversation. We are arguing by the time we are just about a block from the house. He passes our turn, and I ask him where he is going. He tells me to just "shut the hell up!" I know this is beyond bad. We end up near Nocho Park off of Lee Street. I started to say something, but he reared back and slapped me so hard, I'm thinking he must have lost his mind here. I am terrified at this point. I plead with him to let me out of the car. He refuses to do so. I then jump out of the car while it is still moving, and I run up to a house and bang on the door hysterically. A lady came to the door and sees that I am obviously upset. I asked the lady if I could please come in. Thanks be to God, she allowed me to come in. I was so nervous and scared. *I don't know these people, and they must think I'm crazy*, I thought. I calmed after a little while and asked the lady for a ride home. Home was only about two minutes away. She kindly took me home and asked me if I was okay and if I was sure I wanted to go back home. I thanked her and got out of the car.

I have no idea as to how I will get through this, but I know that I will get through by the grace and mercy of God. I pray daily that God will send someone or allow me to cross someone's path that will help me, speak into my life, or come against this life of abuse. The Lord continues to tell me to praise him, and I know he's working things out. I just don't know how. I know things are working for my good regardless of how I'm suffering.

God's word is true, and I believe it no matter what the odds may be!

Chapter 7

Making Another Exit!

I am not able to recall the order of these arguments or fights as they occurred, for you see, there were so many. I know for a period of time I have also suppressed many things until this very day. While I am not able to be certain of the order, I am most certain that the events occurred. All too often, I found myself having to make another exit in order to get away from the preacher and his violent behavior.

We have had another argument, and I run out of the house. My phone had been disconnected, and I need to get to a phone somewhere. It is late at night, and all of the neighbors' lights are off. I continue to run down Watson Street; I run up Lee Street heading east. I know that there's a phone booth there and so I can call the police! Oh, my God! I get there, and the phone cord is broken. I am past the point of fear, because I know he's right behind me. He grabs me and basically escorts me back home. I have no idea as to how bad things may get this time. I remember that short walk home seemed even shorter, because of my own fear of what I would face back at home.

This is a summer day, and I have left home to get away from the preacher. My mother's house is my refuge today. I call a taxi to carry me and my children over there. I am so burdened and so sad. In my heart I need to cry out to and on my mother. I began to weep, and she leads me on the back porch and asks, "What's wrong?" I began to share with her that I just can't take it anymore. I'm wanting to pour it all out, but I can't like I want to, because I know my children are already upset and maybe even listening to what I'm saying. My mother cooks a nice dinner for us, but I can't eat. The children eat and get candy from the candy table. My mother tells me a storm is coming up. I called a minister friend to give us a ride back. On the way home, the rain began to fall very hard and heavy. I arrived home and could not get in; he had locked me out of the house. I insisted on my friend leaving, even though I knew it was thundering and even lightning. I just wanted to be left alone. The kids kept asking questions. I told them we would just sing to the Lord and he would protect us. I knew they were afraid. The preacher had left and locked us out of the house, probably because I had left. He has left home in times past and left that door unlocked so many times before, that I was sure his locking the door was simply spitefulness. A neighbor saw us on the porch and asked if everything was okay. I told her we were just waiting for the preacher to get there to let us in. I prayed he would come soon. With the hard rain, it was starting to get cold and we were very wet. We were all shivering as the rain began to drench our clothing. The wind continued to blow the rain up on the porch under the awning where we were. I think we were on the porch for about an hour before he came; it was not only cold and wet, but also quite dark. Eventually he returned, and his comment to me was that I had no business leaving anyway!

Sometimes I wonder if things could possibly get any worse! Well, they can, and for me things did get worse. Today I have been badgered by the preacher, and I'm feeling so threatened that I had to leave the house. I started walking faster and faster, and suddenly I realized that I was running. I can't see clearly, because my eyes are blinded by my own tears. I feel like I have a mountain in my throat; I can barely swallow. I just want to make it to the church. This is just a short distance up on Gorrell Street. If I can get to the house of God, then everything will be better; I can pray and talk to the Lord. I'm at the church doors, and they are locked. I go to the doors on the side of the church, and they are locked as well. I run to the back, and I am full of anxiety now because I fear the back door will be locked also. I am calling out, but there's no response. Just as I feared, the back door is locked, and there's no one there. I feel so alone and so abandoned. This is one time I feel like I'm the only person in the world going through this hell I'm in!

It's late and it's dark outside, but it does not matter. I feel empty, and I need a resolution to the pain, sorrow, and agony that my life is so full of. It is my children that help to keep a smile on my face and by the grace of God that I continue to put one foot in front of the other each day. Tonight I am tired—tired of the preacher, tired of my children living in this mess I helped to create, and tired of existing. I walk down East Lee Street, and I continue down Morrow Boulevard. My thought process at this time is to locate a box—yes, a box. I'm looking for a box large enough for me to climb inside of. When I find one, I will climb inside of it and not come out for any reason. This will be the place where I sit and die. At this very moment, there were thoughts of my children. Who would raise them in the fear of God? Who would love them as I do and not mistreat them because of who their fathers are? The possible answers to these questions jarred me considerably. I knew that no one would love my children the way I did; I knew that there was no one else who would make certain that they were brought up in the fear of God. I also knew that I wanted my children to live better lives that I had myself! Though I did not wish to live, I wasn't ready to die either, not even mentally! I turned around, and I walked back under the bridge. I began to pray and really talk to God! I really needed his help for my own soundness of mind, and my children needed their mother to be whole!

The word of God lets us know that there is a season for everything, and there will be a time when I will not continue to make another exit. I will not always be in a position of running. It has to get better at some point. God has promised to never leave me nor forsake me, and I choose to believe just that!

Here's another episode I recall! After another heated battle, I know he's going to come for me at some point. I have learned to distinguish a certain look in his eyes. I'm guarded, and I'm braced at this point to exit just in case I need to. Sure enough, he says, "I'll show you something." I immediately run for the door. I run down the steps, down the sidewalk, and down some more steps. I am afraid that I will fall, because I'm filled with fear and I know he is even more angry because I ran out. He's behind me, running just as fast as I am, it seems. I am praying to God to just let me make it to the cab stand. I know those people in there will help me if I just tell them who I am. My great-uncle is the manager; they have to let me in. I am almost there, but he is not far behind, yelling, "Just wait until I catch you. I'm going to get you!"

I reach the cab stand, and I bang on the door as hard as I can. "Let me in. Please let me in. He's going to hurt me." Some lady comes to the door. I said, "Please let me in." She's refusing to allow me to come in. Another lady hears my voice and runs into the room and insists that she let me in. In this moment I just completely lost it; I believe almost every emotion from inside of me came rushing out in the form of tears and grief. I was in pain all over; I didn't seem to have any control over what was going on with me. I knew that I needed to pull myself together, but I was struggling with myself and with what awaited me down the street. My body is trembling. The lady here at the cab stand cannot reach my uncle on the phone, and so she calls the police. One of the ladies walks me to my house, expecting the police to arrive at any moment. The police do come; I'm not sure how long it took. I explained what had happened and that this wasn't the first time, so they suggested a 50B. I still didn't have enough courage or strength to follow through. Not yet!

Chapter 8

Taking a Stand

Thank God I have someone nearby whose home I can take refuge in again. I know I need to leave him, yet I do not believe I have to leave the residence. I need to get in a place where I can hear from God! I need some direction. I have packed enough clothes for my children for a week; I also packed food to take along with us. I was sure to leave little or nothing there for him to eat. I called a friend to pick me up. She has been a witness to some of the trauma I lived. She agrees to help me get the kids from school each day; I make other arrangements to get them to school. During my stay at the evangelist's (my friend's) house, I spend time with God in prayer and in his word. After I had completed what I believed God wanted me to do, I returned home. I believe I was gone for at least several weeks. When my children came in from school on this particular day, I told them we were going back; to them it was home. For me, that house was just a place where I stayed, as long as the preacher was there. We returned, and I knew it would not be easy, but I was ready to confront my fears! I remember the Lord saying to me not to look back this time, as he set me free!

The atmosphere in the house is not much different. However, I am somewhat different after having stayed before God as it relates to my personal struggle with the preacher. The preacher pretends to be working, but as usual, I never see the money. He's supposed to pay the water bill. This is what he would rather do, as opposed to feeling like he's giving me any money. I don't believe he will, but I'll hold out to see if he will. I'm in the kitchen a day or two later, and I hear a vehicle outside. I peep out of the window, and there's a white truck near the house. Since it wasn't in front of the house, I didn't think much of it. As I am rinsing the dishes, the water slowly stops flowing from the faucet. With major frustration, I said, "I knew he wasn't going to pay that bill." I should not be shocked or surprised, but at the same time I'm saying to myself, *I can't believe he would be so cold and uncaring to leave me here with four children and not pay the water bill. He can't even be concerned about his own son to do such a thing.* Not only does he not pay the water bill, he doesn't come back or even call. The preacher probably never planned on paying the bill anyway. He strung me along saying he was going to pay it, and then I get a final notice in the mail. I guess this is his way of not only being sorry and low-down, but also of trying to be in control of what happens to me. Thankfully, the water was off less than twenty-four hours; I had money and was able to pay the bill myself.

You know, there is something called boldness and then there is just plain crazy! When the preacher does return home, he comes with a female—one that I know, by the way. I met her at a church in Raleigh. As a matter of fact, she volunteered to open up her home for my family to stay there one night when the preacher was ministering there some time ago. I always had my suspicions, but I never said a thing about it. She's one among the many. They both play this innocent role; she's just going with him to his court appearance. Mind you, she has a bag with her that says she will be staying overnight. We exchange a few words, and he is on his way out.. The preacher doesn't bother to come back home after court, instead he returns home a few days later, never giving a reasonable explanation as to why he failed to pay the water bill. He couldn't have given me an excuse that would've been acceptable anyway; nothing could justify his actions. When he comes in, he asks if I had cooked. I'm thinking he has to be crazy! All things considered, why ask me if I have cooked? My response was, "No, didn't they have food where you came from?" I knew he was mad, but I could care less, and I was not going to run from him this time. He wanted me to sit down to talk, and I said to him, "I don't care to sit down. I'll just stand and talk."

God as my witness, he became so angry and said, "I said sit down, and that's what I mean," as though I were his child or something. I still refused to sit down. He jumped up out of his chair coming toward me as he always did.

I started feeling quite fearful, and my eyes began to fill with tears. As plain and clear as could be, I heard the voice of God say to me, "Don't let a tear fall from your eyes!" I don't know where the tears went, but I can assure you they never fell from my eyes. As my mother used to say, I guess they rolled back up there. I knew what was about to happen; at this point I felt a sense of surety that I had never felt in dealing with the preacher. He got up in my face and began to just yell. I was not going to be that same victim today. Even if he beat me up, I would not just stand there and take it or just cover my face and protect my head as well. I'm still sure that I wouldn't run this time either. All I know is that he raised his hand to hit me. This time I didn't give him a chance to hit me first; I began to swing on him as I saw his hand going up. I still to this day cannot verbalize how it was that he ended up in the floor on his back with me on top of him. I was beating him as though there were no tomorrow. I don't know who called the police; I just know that they showed up! Two friends of his happened to be there just as the police were coming up and broke up the fight. After the police spoke with both of us and then examined his face, they wanted to arrest me. Can you believe that?! I must say I lit into his behind good, and I felt better because of it. I think I felt some sense of empowerment after this fight. Then I remembered that a few weeks prior to this incident, I had just gotten out of the shower, and I heard the Lord say to me, "I am going to give you some supernatural strength!" I looked at myself in the mirror, as steamed up as it was, and I asked why. It just didn't compute at that time, but I filed it in my mind. This was it! That strength I needed to deal with the preacher without fear!

The end result here was that I shared with the officers the constant abuse that I had been experiencing and the many times I had called the police for help. They checked on the times officers had been dispatched to our address and were able to verify that I spoke the truth about my calling them out. Somehow they found out enough to leave me alone and had the preacher leave the premises. I finally, with the strength of God and courage, went and filed that 50B (restraining order). Our judicial system is not what it used to be, and that is good; however, it needs an overhaul. The preacher was located and apprehended. Unfortunately, by nightfall this man was at my door knocking and calling out to me. I could not believe it! How could this be? I expected for him to be locked up for at least a few days or more. I did exactly as I had been instructed to do, and I called the GPD (Greensboro Police Department). When they arrived, he was trying to get away. Too late! He told them he just wanted to get his clothes. They bought that lie. I put some of his clothes out on the porch, and they all left. A few days later I had gone to church service. I noticed as I was coming up to the house that my porch light was out. I knew for sure I had turned it on as I was leaving. I asked the sister I was riding with to wait until I had got inside and made sure everything was okay. I remember the children were asleep. The sitter was fine and left to go home. About an hour or so later as I was in bed, I kept hearing strange noises, but I couldn't tell where the noises were coming from. Eventually, I fell off to sleep. Sometime later I awakened suddenly, and there was the preacher standing over me. I don't know that I have ever been so messed up. I couldn't think fast enough. I'm taken. He must have been hiding outside of the house somewhere and damaged the lightbulb so that I could not see him. Without truly processing each thought, I'm thinking, *How did he get in here? What does he want? What is he going to do?* Only God would get me through this. I jumped up and went for the phone; of course he had gotten it already. He said he just wanted to talk. I felt as though I had no choice. He talked about how sorry he was and how he needed for me to take him back. He was so depressed, and he went on and on; he was weighing in on me as the hour was growing late. I seem to grow weaker by the minute. I had to catch myself to be sure I didn't say something I didn't really mean just to get him to hurry up and leave. He left after several grueling hours. He begged me not to call the police on him. I made it clear to him that he was not to return or I would call them.

On a cold and brisk night, I had put the kids to bed rather early, as I usually did during the winter. I fell asleep on the living room sofa. I awakened suddenly and sat straight up on the sofa. I heard a noise on my left, and there was the preacher coming in through the sliding glass door. I know the Lord awakened me just in time. I ran out of the door and called the police from a neighbor's phone. Of course, by the time the police arrived he was long gone. My nerves were shot for the rest of the night, and for a while after that. Things were so bad with him refusing to give up that I had friends stay over with me sometimes or stay as long they could into the night. I didn't really have a chance to recover before he was at it again. The preacher was so bad off, that not only did he stalk me, but he also had another man follow me around as well! I was in such a state of unbelief. He cannot be functioning with a sound mind. A person with a sound mind would not demonstrate these types of behaviors. Therefore, I became even more cautious of him. I'm not certain as to how many times he broke into the house while we were asleep; I'm sure it was more than four. Each time I called the police, but if he was caught, he managed to be out of jail within twenty-four to forty-eight hours. I felt like it was a type of game or something to him. The judicial system is another story altogether.

The kids are preparing for bed; I'm cleaning up the kitchen. I think I hear something but cannot be sure. The area is known for late-night walkers, so I don't dwell on it. Later, one of the kids said to me they thought they heard someone around the back of the house. We didn't have a back door, so there was no way to look out and see. I thought it was the late-night traffic, as they were known for walking through a path that led along the side of the house and around to the back. After the kids were all in bed and asleep, I continued to pick up around the house, careful to listen for any noises. I decided to go into the living room and just listen, but I heard nothing. The telephone rang, and I answered; I began to talk with a friend. While having this conversation, I kept hearing a funny noise—one I couldn't quite figure out what it could be. It sounded like movement of some kind, but strangely so. I told the person that I was speaking with what I heard. I also told her I thought that noise could be coming from underneath the house. This was crazy! I finish my call and continue to listen to the noise under the house. I now know for sure the preacher is the one under the house. It had to be the preacher! I decide to call the police. I went out the front door and across the street and called the police. I was careful to open the door quietly, and I left it cracked instead of closing it all the way. Talk about somebody running fast there and back—I made that trip so quickly it blew my own mind. I felt so good once I was back inside with the door closed and locked. Thinking he could break in didn't matter to me at all.(He would've had to literally bust the windows or something, because a bishop friend of mine had come over and nailed all of the windows shut so I could feel safe and sleep at night.) All I knew was that the police were on their way, and no matter what, I could be okay until they were here. In just a short period of time, there was a knock at the door. Even though I hoped it was the police, I made no assumptions; with my voice nervous and somewhat cracked, I yelled out to ask who it was. The response was, "The Greensboro Police Department." Oh, my God! I felt heaviness begin to lift right then. They came in, and I explained what had taken place. They told me to lock the door and have the kids go into their rooms. Four or five police officers went around the back. I listened from the back of the house, and I could hear them talking, but I didn't understand what was being said. They commanded the preacher to come out—this I heard. You know, I wasn't really shocked, but I said, *What?* to myself! *Can you believe this?* The police spoke with him and consequently took him to jail for a short stay, as usual. He had lime all over his clothes; I had seen that on him before but made no connection with his being beneath the house. Now I realized that the time before when I saw him looking so dusty, he had been under the house. He had asked me previously about something that he heard I said. He told the truth. He heard me firsthand, because he was under the house crawling around as I moved about with the cordless phone. That was completely obsessive and insane, and evil! I'm sure if I were more acquainted with medical terms I could add another diagnosis. Can you believe it? Under my house. This man has major problems: he has followed me himself, had someone else follow me, hid out under my house, unscrewed my porch lightbulb, hid on the side of the house, and suddenly appeared.

Here is what did it: The children and I had gone out for the evening with a friend of mine. When we arrived back home, it was quite foggy. My eldest son was known for saying the most unusual things and seeing what we couldn't see. The preacher had gotten a van from someone, saying he was going to fix it and transport people to church. Well, as you may know, he never did. We were in the car just chatting before I took the kids inside. My son says, "Momma, it's a man in the van."

I said, "What?"

"It's a man in the van," he repeated.

"There's not a man in the van," I said.

"Yes it is, Momma," he said. He was very adamant about it, so I decided to take note without making everyone else aware that I was gazing as hard as I could. It was hard to see, because not only was it foggy, but it was dark as well. Oh, my goodness. I saw a man and knew that it was the preacher by his head. We sat there awhile, and I tried to figure out what to do. I knew that I should call the police, but that just wasn't working, obviously. I asked my eldest son's father to come over, and he did, with my sister's boyfriend. He told us to go inside, and they went up to the van. He opened the van door, and there was the preacher, trying to hide! My son's father told him to bring his behind on out of there. He came out just as scared as he could be; he wasn't expecting him.

My son's father made the preacher come inside the house; he actually pushed him in because he was so slow about going in. He told the preacher, "You want to fight? You have a man now, so fight me instead of being a punk and hitting on a woman." As sad as it was, the preacher was just as cowardly-acting as he could be. As the older folks would say, "Tell the truth and shame the devil." Let me tell you, I was glad for him to be getting what he had dished out. I know I was wrong as I could be, but in that moment I wanted him to feel some of what I had felt. (I wasn't thinking about vengeance belonging to God.) All of this happened after this preacher had been warned not to ever come back. I must say that when he did come back, he was peaceable; however, I refused to speak with him. Thank God, he finally got the message. What sweet relief. He never came back after this; he called, of course. As a matter of fact, on one occasion he called me and asked me if I thought there was a chance we would ever get back together. That warranted a very matter-of-fact no, leaving no room for hope as far as I was concerned. He then asked me if I would file for divorce, because he was going to get married! I could not believe, first of all, that he had the gall to ask me to file for a divorce because he was engaged, and second, how he could be planning to get married so quickly. I told the Lord, *I sure hope someone tells whoever she is what she's about to get herself into.* For a moment I wished I knew who she was, hoping I could spare her some of the pain and agony that I experienced. I did pray for her. I prayed that God would cause her eyes to be opened and that she would not allow him to treat her the way he had treated me. Learning that her father was a pastor, I felt for sure her father would see through him so quickly. Unfortunately not—they later married!

Chapter 9

A Collective View

"A Collective View" is a collection of the views of others that witnessed some of the events that took place regarding my abuse. Some of the writers also share how they were adversely affected as a result of witnessing the abuse.

He played a good game; I thought that he loved my sister and her kids. I remember my sister calling my mother, telling her that he had beat her on one occasion. I also recall that during the time I was living a fast lifestyle, I had a friend whose cousin was into the homosexual lifestyle. My friend and I would go to this guy's house (homosexual). One day I was there and the guy I'll call "J" was telling us that he had a man. A few days later we were at "J's" apartment and there was a knock at the door; "J" said, "See, I told ya'll I had a man!" I was shocked because it was the preacher. I said to my friend that it was my sister's husband. He looked at me as if he could not believe it was me. "J" had told us how the preacher would tell my sister he was going to church; he would throw clothes out of the bathroom window and get them as he left the house. When he got where he was going, he would change.

Later in talking with my mother, she said "that so and so I could beat his you know what! (She was talking about the preacher.) I told my mother, "Come on. Let's go over and beat his tail." We got a ride over to their house.

My mother at a point said, "It's time." We lit into his butt; we whipped on his behind. His mother came after it was all over and invited us to fight her; my mother was ready. The man who gave us a ride grabbed her. His mother called me some names, and I let her know that I don't talk back to grown people! He called the police, thinking they were going to arrest us and take us to jail. They had a warrant out for his arrest. So they took him to jail! He was no good for my sister at all.

Thank God she has a good husband now!

Brenda J. Albright

Meeting Marva and the preacher was a great turnaround in my life, in reference to good friends and ministry. It seemed to have been a wonderful beginning. This family seemed to love each other and walked closely in ministry. The preacher was a singer, a prophet, and a musician. I watched his wife stand with him every step of the way. She mothered their children (one his and the others before the marriage) and was a wife to him. I witnessed this on many occasions.

My daughter and I became mutual friends with their family. At first, I didn't realize that there was a problem. This was a loving family. Later, I saw that something was wrong here. One day when I came over to visit as usual, I perceived that there was a spirit of rage. Marva came from the back of the house; she did all she could to cover her husband and to hide her emotions. But that particular day was the beginning of her being able to tell someone else what was going on.

I thought, She's a woman of God; I wonder how long she's been going through such acts of violence and abuse. I knew that she needed someone by her with the help of God to help her get through this. I was concerned for the children and their well-being. I knew that abuse was wrong—it did not matter where it came from. I wanted to make sure that help was there. I knew that God would take her through; she was a strong woman of God! I speak to her strength because for so long she endured this without anyone on the outside knowing what was going on in her home life.

I could not understand how such an anointed vessel of God could behave in such a manner as this; the preacher was anointed. You just never know about people; you never know who's who. You never know who's suffering or to what degree they are suffering. I have learned through this experience not to put my confidence in man but to trust in God. We must not close our eyes to ungodliness. In knowing these two at that time, I met many prophets, male and female alike. I know that they had to close their eyes to the ungodliness that went on. I think about the danger that she was in and that no one stood up for her or stepped up to the plate to rescue her and her children. When I say this, I mean men and women of God who had the means and the influence to do so. We must not be moved by gifts and callings, as they are without repentance. We must look for the fruit in their lives.

God bless each and every reader of this book. I believe it to be amazing.

Cynthia Clark, Evangelist,

I will reflect on my memories and try to put them in some kind of order to create as accurate a picture of my feelings and experience as possible.

I remember those days as a time when I often felt more was going on than I knew. I'm so glad I had the Holy Ghost, because in those times I was very naive.

On a few occasions I remember in particular, we entered the home to be faced with a thickness in the air that could not be denied. Sometimes, even my children noticed something seemed amiss. It had to be my inexperience that gave cover to the bishop, for it seems to me now and shortly after I found out the truth, that it was all a show put on for my benefit. Minister Davis knew but was not at liberty to expose the truth, because it wasn't her truth to tell.

I remember with clarity the day I found out the truth. My children and I went to church as was our custom, and upon entering the house I discerned a thickness in the atmosphere that wouldn't be denied. The service moved on as per the program, but all were not at ease, especially me. Finally, the bishop spoke a word or phase that caused the Spirit of God in me to say (loudly), Leave! Without delay I got my kids, and we left. We actually walked home. All the way home I questioned the Spirit, but it wasn't until Evangelist Marva came to my home later that day that I understood it all. She began to tell me the very sad story of her pain and the suffering of her and her family. I cried out in pain because someone I loved was going through such horror. The pain was greater because it came by the hand of another that I loved and trusted. I never got into not forgiving him, because I felt pity for the payment I saw he'd have to pay. I left the ministry at the church because I no longer respected the man; I loved him, but I couldn't follow him!

I'll sum up my feelings by saying this: I hate that I was too naive to see clearly what was going on, because it continued because I remained in darkness. The truth had to come out, but had I been more on my game, it would not have gone on as long as it did. Ignorance is truly no excuse!

I learned from this experience and therefore count it all joy, but only in the light that God brings us out of all things if we would but trust him!

Your sister in Christ,

Anthonette Morehead

As I thought long and hard, even often about what I would say about that time in our life, it was this:

You asked what were my thoughts about the bishop.

And they were this:

I knew nothing about what was happening to cause the rage that was within, if anything. I just knew it existed. I only looked on him as an anointed vessel of God, because of what I saw behind the pulpit, not what I heard behind the closed door. I was fairly new in the Lord and believed what I was told and what the word said about obeying them that had the rule over me, and he was always careful never to let me see anything that would cause me to lose faith in him. He was always careful to say the famous words, "Look what you made me do and I have to go and minister to God's people." So I guess you could say, I looked at his ministry (the spiritual) and not his personal life (the natural). That is why I stayed.

I never thought that there was anything that Evangelist Marva did to cause anything that happened. I truly separated them from what they did there could ever be a cause. I believed that she was holding on to dear life to the word of God and what you believed was pleasing in his sight. I can say that what hurt me was to see what you were going through. I felt your pain as you continued, no matter what had just occurred, to remain godly toward him and those that were there. Those same people he classically called "God's people." It actually has made me respect you more. I often questioned God as to why I had to witness that. It was painful enough for you, but to have people hear it (the things that were said) I knew made it more painful.

I remember me and Minister M going and speaking with another bishop after we had disbanded about us leaving the church, and what he said was that you were always given to prophecy. I asked him what that meant, and he basically said that you pretty much at that time believed whatever prophecy was given to you, and that I was faithful to a fault to my own hurt, and that was why we stayed so long. It makes me believe now that perhaps he may have been one of the ones God spoke to, and he never said anything to you or even us.

We made it through! In addition to what I've said already, after more soul-searching, I have come to this understanding about myself. I was looking through the eyes of an abused person, being abused myself; I have had some controlling and abusive person in my life as far as I can remember, beginning with my very own father. He always made me feel inferior and not quite good enough. Then as I began to date and even to gather friends, I attracted the same kinds of people into my life. I even married a man that has tried on many occasions, by my own admissions controlled me.

Having admitted this to myself, I must also admit that even as an adult, I was not a good judge of what was, or what should have been acceptable. I knew right from wrong and how I wanted to be treated. I think that because of my own abuse, I never felt or thought that things were as bad as they really were. I couldn't see it! I always thought the Lord would fix whatever was broken. During the time that now Pastor Marva was going through such turmoil, I had the bishop whispering in my ear one thing, and others whispering something else. The bishop would often use the quote "the Lord said" as a way to get me to tell Pastor Marva what he thought I should tell her and say it was from the Lord. I never allowed myself to do that, though. My husband told me that one day I would see the truth about the bishop! So to say that I was torn was an understatement. How do you go against God and one you believe to be the man of God? I now understand how he used my love for him and my love for God against me. These have been very painful acknowledgments. In dealing with the pain of mistrust, with the help of God, healing has begun and I can begin to trust.

Again.

Minister Sybil Davis

Things are different everywhere you go; being at my sister Marva's with my two girls was good in some ways and difficult in others. My two children and her five were some experience (the husband was as a child himself) and could be taxing at moments. The "real children" got along fine. They enjoyed the walks to the park, as did

1. It was breathing time, and we all needed that. The sergeant (playing preacher) walked around giving orders, but I dared not say a word, and it was because I was in their house.

Sometimes he'd have a cruel word or way with my sister or the children. I thought of locking him outside of the house or even nailing the windows shut so he couldn't throw his clubbing clothes out of the window with such ease. I guess everyone has a side we don't know or understand. He was preaching in the day and clubbing at night. Everybody is different—God remains the same. I wondered if Marva knew he was going to the club.

Wanda K. Johnson

I remember getting a phone call from Marva one night, she said that the preacher had been hitting on her. My son was not around at the time, I decided to over to their house alone. After I arrived there, I rang the doorbell and Iarva let me inside. The preacher came into the kitchen and living room area. He asked me what did I want and what was I going to do. I remember telling him that if he put his hands on my niece again that I was going to beat him with a bat. He responded by saying that I wasn't going to do a thing to him with sarcasim. I then asked Marva if she was okay and she said that she was. I also asked her if she wanted to leave but she said no!

Phyliss Malone, Aunt

When my mother was married to him I remember not liking him right away. I was mad at him for taking her and not letting her come back home till the day after my birthday. I also remember my biological father telling him to never put his hands on me and if he ever did that he would kill him, and you know what? He never touched me. I appreciate my mother for everything. I think that you go through things so that they make you stronger and at times I Wished that it never had to be as bad and traumatic. I feel as though he took something so major from my mother however God gave her something even greater. Not all abusive situations end like the way that my mother's did, she came out alive. So many women die each year from domestic violence. I have a very strong mother who loves life but loves God even more and I know that it's because of him and his plan for her life that she is where she is at today considering where she has come from.

I remember I use to say that when I got older I was going to beat him up worse than he beat my mother. I was going to sock it to him. I now know that I can't do that but at times I still want to. I still need prayer. ;) I just don't like seeing him now because at times it seems as if he has no regret or no remorse. However it's God that knows our heart and he will have to answer to his past and wrong doings if he hasn't already. I just know that he will never lay another hand on my family.

I appreciate all the wise words and those words of encouragement that my mother had for us because I feel that even though she came out of it she helped us to come out of it also by being an amazing mother and an even better praying warrior. I am glad to have a Mother like her and wouldn't trade her for anything. All that we have gone through in the past has brought us to where we are now. Thank you mamas for being an excellent role model and you have been and will always be an inspiration in my life forever and always Love.

Khatara A. Johnson, daughter

As I reflect back I can recognize that my early childhood life was mostly spent in a broken home. Although there were both good and bad times that I remember, what stands out is the unhappiness and hurt. Not solely within myself, but within my family. Many people knew him as Bishop …., but living with him was knowing him in a totally different way. I can recall times when Phillip and my mother would appear to be happy, enjoying life, but then other times they were arguing and literally wrestling around in their bedroom and in the living room. I can remember seeing my mother trying with all her might to fight back, and saying to myself, "when I get bigger I'm gonna get him back".

There is one incident I do remember very well, I believe mostly because of the hurt, embarrassment and anger that I felt as a child. Coming home from school one day, I can remember the driver pulling up right in front of our house and seeing my mother and him on the porch arguing, and he restraining my mother. I held my head down in shame as I got off the bus, what could I do but cry, and hope that he would just stop. It's a terrible feeling as a child to see the one person you love most being hurt and you know there's nothing you can do.

I don't remember much from this time in my life but I learned a lot from this situation. It stands out in my mind when I think of settling down and having a family of my own. It's amazing how something that happened so long ago can affect a person their entire life. I will always remember this and the pain the family endured because of it. I know I don't want to go through it myself and no woman should ever have to. I know the signs to look for and what not to just ignore. It's a lesson learned, today I'm more cautious because of it.

I can remember not really having a relationship with my mother until after it was just her and my three siblings. During the time where he was present there was an obvious discomfort. When he left it was then when we were a family and we were able to bond. I can remember lying in my mother's bed, talking, and praying with her. This was the time where I can really recall the growth and bond in our relationship. My mother is incredibly strong, she has endured so much, and I'm truly proud to have her as my mother. Without her I really don't know where I would be. She has had such an impact on my life and for that I'm so appreciative.

I am also very appreciative for the man I call "Pops". He came into our lives years ago and although it was rocky in the beginning he has proved to be a man of great character. I respect him for being the man that he is and taking care of my mother as she deserves. Not only has this man taken care of his wife but also her four children, he has been a great father and mentor. As I have come of age I appreciate more and more the things my mother and Pops have done for me and I don't take it lightly, you are truly a blessing, I love you both very much!

KieSharra

Chapter 10

Hurt People Hurt People!

We have all heard it said that hurt people do hurt people. As much as I wanted to remain angry at the preacher, it was because of my own healing and deliverance that I was able to forgive him and to have compassion toward him. I must acknowledge that I have lived out the truth of "hurt people, hurt people." While I make no excuses for the preacher, I yet recognize that when we are hurt, without proper support and without a will or proper guidance to move forward, we will do to others what has been done to us, and possibly even more. The pain of what has happened to a victim wreaks another evil when not dealt with appropriately. I think because of the need to have some control, finally some of those who have been abused become controlling and eventually abusive—verbally, emotionally, and/or physically.

The preacher was certainly abused as a child, based on what he shared with me previously and what I learned from others who knew him. This was some years after we had gone our separate ways and had no contact with one another. I am sure his abuse was never properly addressed, by him or by other authority figures in his life, then or prior to my having met him. I believe he masked his hurt and pain by engaging in other unhealthy and inappropriate activities and repeating the cycle of abuse. I learned that before he met me, he had abused one of his daughters. In my questioning him after I heard about it, he denied what was then an allegation being made. Because of all of the abuse I had suffered at his hands, I knew he had abused his daughter. At some point after our breakup, I found documents that detailed the nature of his daughter's abuse. It spoke of the welts that bled upon her body and other bruising that resulted from being beaten. The preacher spoke of how he was beaten with extension cords, iron cords, and very large switches. Considering that the preacher was beaten with inappropriate objects, whether he was beaten at home or in foster care, it's no surprise that he inflicted the same type of maltreatment upon his daughter, me, and perhaps even others. There were times that I could look into the preacher's eyes and see the evil. It was as though a transformation took place in him right before my very eyes. I imagine that a part of this rage was a result of the abuse he encountered himself.

Rage is a very common characteristic for those who have suffered abuse. I think what's worse is not knowing how to control the rage rather than being controlled by the rage itself. Rage will always employ another victim! True it is that "hurt people do hurt people."

In all of the preacher's abusiveness, there was still some good inside of him, as it is within each of us. He was truly gifted of God. He played the organ with great skill and joy. As I remember, he loved to just sit and play the Hammond organ. Because of his growing up in the church, he knew songs that most of us had maybe only heard of, and he also sang them very well. When it came to preaching, he did a great job in his delivery of the word. He had a way of drawing people and causing a congregation to become excited and to feel a sense of being empowered. As it concerned his children, I know that he loved them as best as he knew how at that time. You can only give out of what you have; you can only work with what you have, and God can only do in us what we allow!

Although the preacher was gifted and talented, we must realize the need for integrity also in doing the work of the Lord. There has to be a lifestyle that is in accordance with the word of God. We must allow the whole of our being to be taken care of or to be ministered to in order to be healthy spiritually and to therefore have a positive impact on the lives of others.

Being gifted is not enough! Each of us must allow the Holy Spirit to rule in our lives; if we have accepted Jesus as Lord and Savior, then it should be our desire for him to rule in our lives! This certainly isn't to suggest that we won't fall or come short of God's glory, because surely we will, yet we strive and desire for his will to be done in our lives. I believe the preacher lost sight of his purpose as a result of his not dealing with the inner pain and struggles that he had experienced. I believe that he found some level of comfort for his pain, and that comfort developed into his becoming attached to the things of the world and consequently taking on more qualities unlike those of the Lord. Perhaps he even lost the ability to focus on his purpose, something that can happen to anyone. We must be prayerful and watchful as we pursue the things of God, knowing that we are being pursued by the devil. Be healed, be set free, and be delivered by the power of the one and only true and living God! I believe that it is only upon healing and deliverance that we can move forward in a healthy way, enabling ourselves to be used for the glory of God. Outside of this, I think we position ourselves to be further victimized or to victimize others. There's a need that many fail to meet in their own Christian journey. That is the need to be mentored and the need to have been covered (shepherded; having true accountability) as a believer in the body of Christ. (Submitting to proper leadership is vital.) It is my prayer for the preacher that he will be strengthened and encouraged to confront the issues that have caused him hurt; in this perhaps he can cease to hurt others. It is the will of God that none be lost, but rather that all be saved! Despite the agony he brought to the lives of my children and myself, I pray for the preacher to be totally set free from the things that have him bound. Only then will he have a heart change and the mind-set to refrain from hurting other people and altering their lives in such a damaging way!

Chapter 11

The Power of Abuse!

Abuse is very scary, very painful. The power of abuse brings about life-changing experiences. With many negative experiences and the days and nights I lived being somewhat consumed by fear, my life changed over and over again. I continued in a state of increasing fear, trying to exercise the power of prayer and trying to trust God with all that was within me. I felt that with each new but negative experience, I lost more and more of who I was. It has always been my thought and my opinion that there are few people who have never experienced abuse, but yet understand the process and the power of it and how it can be difficult for one to leave that abusive situation. Difficult, but not impossible!

"Criticism comes easy as we look from the outside in, however, to the person who looks from the inside out, criticism is mostly what they live." I know that there were many people who were angry with me and thought that I was just crazy for not leaving the preacher long before I did. The truth is that I wanted to leave long before I did! Oftentimes, people don't realize that abuse is truly a process, and unless you are familiar with the process, it's very easy to miss the signs of an abuser or of one who is being abused. Abuse in many cases is very carefully thought out—a slow, methodical, and gradual process. That being the case, a victim usually doesn't realize that they are being pursued in such a negative manner. For many, being pursued says, I'm desirable and he or she really likes me. In my case, I didn't realize that I was being abused until I had to ask myself, "Where am I?" after a major blow to my head and to my face. Other things had occurred, but this is when the light came on for me. The problem was that by then I was very much a victim; I had become broken. Being broken is defined as "violently separated, into parts, destroyed, or damaged or altered by breaking." My life was shattered indeed, and I was overcome with fear. With my family relationships having such varying degrees of closeness, and knowing that some of the women in my family had suffered domestic violence, I wasn't sure how to handle my own situation. In addition to that, I was literally afraid of what some of them would have done had they known the depth of what I was suffering at the preacher's hand. My brokenness caused me to lack good judgment in some situations—another example of the power of abuse. I needed to be free and to be made whole again.

Despite my own sufferings and my running scared at a very vulnerable and lonely point in my life, because of the power of abuse, I was too often more concerned about the needs of others than about my own needs. Because of this, my own needs continued to go unmet. This, coupled with the constant abuse—whether verbal, mental, or physical—was a true recipe for disaster in my own life. In my brokenness, I hadn't realized how weak and fragile I had become. I had always been a person who stood up for herself; I was outspoken at times and not at all easily intimidated. Over time, these qualities were replaced with being taking advantage of, being afraid to speak at times out of fear of retribution, and being easily intimidated by the preacher. It was as though I looked up one day and wasn't sure as to whom I had become. I remember not wanting to look at myself in the mirror for extended periods of time, because I did not like the person that I had become. I came to think less and less of myself, while I was being abused more and more. As I remember now what were red flags for me, it is easy to see how the game was being played. I was being groomed for the preacher to use as he willed. My limits were being tested, and because I permitted so much, the preacher saw no limits for himself where I was concerned. It is important to always have boundaries and standards that you uphold for yourself and to live in a way that others honor, or at least respect! "Red flags" are red flags for a reason. If one is blind to the red flags, then to that person they don't exist! There were many red flags that I never saw.

Victims are often reluctant to cry out for help because of the criticism and lack of understanding from those they love and trust. This can lead to an extended stay in a very dangerous situation. For me, I was embarrassed, humiliated, and ashamed of my situation. Though I knew it wasn't my fault, I still felt like it was. It was difficult to come to trust enough to completely open up and tell others about the preacher's "true colors," as they were many. Given time, a person's true colors will shine through, sometimes when they are not even aware of it. The preacher's true colors were alarming to me; they were not colors of a man of God and not those of one proclaiming the office of bishop. I remember my late bishop, Bishop J. H. Covington, telling us to check out the parents of the person we were involved with. He said we should get to know the family, among other things. Somehow, I lost sight of that valuable piece of information. Had I done this, I would have had more information, maybe even sparing myself some of the heartache I endured. Praise the Lord. I'm free!

Because of my embarrassment and my desire to preserve the ministry and to protect the church members, so I thought, I covered my wounds. "Wounds do need to be protected in a number of cases, however in others, they need to be exposed so that they can be aired allowing the healing process to begin as a result of being exposed." Because I took this route, I think I kept myself bracing for battle; there was always another fight to prepare for and another argument to be had. I should have exposed the evil I lived with much sooner.

I remember the first time I came home crying because a girl had hit me a couple of times while we were playing outside. When my mother inquired as to why I was crying, I told her what had happened. She sent me back where I came from and told me not to come back until I found the girl and hit her back. While it may have some harshness, the lesson was to always take up for yourself. Don't go running or allow others to take advantage of you. My mother was a strong disciplinarian and a strong woman. With my having been taught that, I still found myself making another exit, running away from my attacker. Although many of my exits were physical, I made many mental exits just to free my mind and to have an escape from the torment at times. The Lord promised to give us a way of escape when what we are confronted with is more than we can withstand! (Paraphrased). There hath no temptation taken you but such as is common to man: but God is faithful, who will not suffer you to be tempted above that ye are able; but will with the temptation also make a way to escape, that ye may be able to bear it.

There should come a time in each of our lives that we grow tired of running and making exits out of fear. We must find ourselves taking a stand with the help of God. It is never the will of our God that we are mistreated or abused in any way, although it does happen. I had to pray fervently for God to help me to take a stand in the face of evil. I cannot say that anything about this experience was easy, because it never was. I continued to learn to trust God in ways I never had before. I learned to pray in a way that I had never prayed before, and I learned how to wait on God when it seemed as though I could die before he came to see about me! I lived to get free from the chains that had me bound, and thank goodness that my mind is sound. In that, I'm very blessed by God!

In relationships we sometimes become smitten, in love, emotionally involved, or even sexually involved, such that our judgment may be clouded. We sometimes fail to really search out the individual we are involving ourselves with. The fact that I allowed these things to happen in my life (with my being a confident, not easily intimidated, and balanced Christian) demonstrates how we can go into a faraway place emotionally; we can become too carefree, enjoying the moment and failing to ask or take note of the important things that tell us who a person really is, or what really speaks to the individual's true character. I believe that almost every time we move to a new place in life or experience a new relationship, it has a honeymoon period. During that time, there's pure enjoyment and bliss. After this time has passed, the emotions run deep and expectations are reasonable or not are set. While we may have learned some things, we haven't had enough time to know many other things that make up the person. I never knew the extent of emotional and physical hurt that the preacher had experienced until I had overcome my abuse from him. While I do not hold the preacher blameless, I do accept that because of his own abuse, he repeated the cycle with those he knew he could prey upon. If his intended prey was not in his circle, then he did everything he could possibly do to graft them into his circle. Why? Because "hurt people hurt people."

Many nights I cried, and I even asked God why. I prayed, and I prayed some more. I even tried to pray differently in hopes of a quick resolution to my problem. The beatings continued, but so did my faith in God. I believed in him more because I had less and less. I heard the counsel of preachers and other leaders in the house of God. Some of that counsel was good, and then some of it was bad. As a matter of fact, I had a prophet tell me, "If you don't allow the preacher to come home, then God is going to curse you."

I responded by saying, "I'll have to be cursed then!" I was not about to allow him to return home this time! I prayed, and I kept moving! I cannot stress the importance of knowing the voice of God for yourself, and trusting God! You see, the Lord had released me from the preacher once before, and I allowed another preacher to convince me to take him back. Not twenty-four hours had passed before I knew that I had made a dreadful mistake. The Lord let me to know that I would have to suffer for that. He had already spoken to me, and I followed the lead of someone else. This person wasn't being the mouthpiece of God, but rather, he was speaking out of himself. This was to my own detriment, and it was from the enemy who wished to destroy me in any way possible. Today, I glorify God because he allowed me to be strengthened that I could overcome that mountain in my life.

Chapter 12

Bound to Be Free

Bound to be free—that's me! I was bound to be free because there were people praying for me; I was bound to be free because Christ died that I might be free. I was bound to be free with Jesus living inside of me. I knew that God had a purpose for me. I remember that when I was pregnant with my eldest son, my late bishop, Bishop J. H. Covington, ministered to me, and he told me that the Lord said he had a purpose for me and that he was going to make me an example to young people and raise me up and cause me to be blessed. He said that this child would cause me to be blessed as well. I had to try to keep reminding myself of positive things to make it through. Listening to music by Yolanda Adams always encouraged me; her current music at that time reached my soul and ministered to me in that moment. It didn't change what I was going through, but it certainly did help me to make it through! This too shall pass—oh how that song blessed me, among other songs of hers and other artists. Thank God for creativity in ministering healing, comfort, and deliverance through the word of God.

It's Friday, and there's a revival ending at St. Mark Holiness Church; the woman of God preaching tonight is Prophetess Marilyn Griffith. I've heard her quite a few times before, and I feel the need to be in church tonight, so I prepare to attend the service. During the service the power of God was moving mightily! I prayed for God to speak to me; I felt that sense of desperation. I said to God, "I need to hear from you!" The woman of God began to move out in my direction, and I could feel the anointing of God upon me. Suddenly the atmosphere changed. After a few minutes it was all quite clear—the preacher had come in. After the service was over, I hurried to the car with the person I rode with, and I went home. On Sunday evening, Prophetess Griffith was preaching at another church, Gospel Feast. I went to the service, having every confidence that God would speak to me; I was in such a delicate place, and I need God's help. The service was going on nicely. After the word of God was ministered, the woman of God asked for the congregants to come up for prayer, and many of them did. I wanted to go, but I found it difficult to move my feet. Finally, I was able to move. As I began to move out of my seat, our spirits connected and I knew that God was speaking to her. By this time, I am in the aisle and tears are streaming down my face. When I was halfway down the aisle, she asked me what I wanted prayer for. My response was, "Just pray. Just pray for me."

She began to say, "Oh God. Oh God," and then she told me the Lord said that there was a corporate conspiracy against me and that the devil was trying to destroy me. She ministered other things as well that spoke directly to my current situation. I knew that God had heard my cry and that he knew what was in my heart that I could not say. In that hour, I experienced some true healing and deliverance from the bondage that I had been in. I truly did not leave the same way I came! My God had laid his hands on me, and I was bound to be free!

Regardless of the degree to which I suffered, I always held out hope and trust that God would somehow make a way of escape for my children and me. It would not be wrong to say I hoped against hope. Sometimes it looked as though the change would never come. I had to remind myself about some of the things that had been spoken into my life that I knew were of God. In the worst of times, we must trust God. It doesn't mean that I never felt like giving up—you know by now that I did, but it was only for that moment in a passing thought. When our hearts are turned toward God, he never leaves us without a means to escape. In other words, he always makes a way for us to be in a safe place; that place is in him. But he also opens doors and makes resources available to us that we must access. This doesn't happen when we want it to necessarily, but in God's appointed time. Being tangled up in any abusive situation has a way of distorting one's thinking and judgment to some degree. You often times lose sight of good judgment or clarity of thoughts. I could have chosen to leave. I didn't do that. For me, the preacher ended up having to leave the residence. I had already left him in my heart a long time ago, as it was my desire to be free.

In my quest to be free, I met many people and was shunned by many more. There were people who chose not to deal with me because of the preacher, those who thought less of me and my walk with God because I had dealt with the preacher, those who whispered and stared when they realized who I was, and then those who just didn't know what to do. With the strength of God as my help, I overcame those things very quickly. What was difficult to overcome after the preacher was no longer there and the marriage was annulled, was hearing any part of his name. (The marriage was annulled because the preacher had been married previously; he was separated but never divorced.) He had actually been married to the daughter of a pastor. I better understood why he wanted to go to outside of North Carolina for a marriage license. I realized how much more I had been damaged by him and all concerning him. Day by day, I see how much my life had been torn apart; my children had been touched by domestic violence forever. I would never be able to remove the images from their minds, nor the words that had been spoken. He was just so full of lies and deceptions—not to mention my own poor decision making. I had to be true to myself and acknowledge how I needed prayer. I needed to be somewhat taken by the hand to enable the process of being free to start becoming more of a reality for me and mine! I struggled and I struggled; I cried and I cried. I would wait for the children to go to bed and then just release some of the agony and pain that I carried inside. While the preacher may have been gone, I still felt his presence, and quite strongly at that. This brought about fear in me. I associated feeling his presence with the possibility of his suddenly appearing at any moment. So many things raced through my mind. So as it was, he's no longer there but yet having so much control in my life. The more I prayed from a sincere heart and the more I spent time in the word of God, the more confidence I gained in the freedom I wanted to live in. I accepted the fact that the only control he could have was that that I allowed him to have. The control was over. I was no longer afraid of him, I no longer felt threatened by him, and I chose to no longer deal with him. I made a decision to not ask him for any child support.

The time came when we had to appear in court because of the restraining order I had taken out. I don't recall ever having been so nervous in all of my life! Being before a judge was a big deal, despite the fact I hadn't committed a crime. The judge honored the restraining order. I remember the judge asking about child support, and I made it clear that I didn't want any from the preacher. He encouraged me to pursue it later on, as it was the preacher's obligation to provide child support for his own child. I didn't want any child support monetarily or in any capacity; I just simply wanted the preacher to completely *vanish* from my life. I didn't need or want anything from him at all. I was moving closer and closer to that point of being free, in more ways than one, and I wanted nothing to interfere with that process.

With my life now on a different path, with much prayer and time spent in the word of God, I'm able to see daily my own brokenness, my fragility, and even my vulnerability. Yes, I was in a process of healing, but I was still seeing more clearly the truth about where I really was. There I was once again, still needing so much myself, but making sure that I was there for someone else. (I realize now how that was a flaw in my character. I was helping others oftentimes out of a need or a cry for help myself.) Unfortunately, at this time I was not surrounded by people who cared enough to nurture me back to a healthy place, or by people who were able to. Regardless of the situation, I had to pray for the strength of God and seek out ways to keep myself encouraged. What an incredible task this was. Getting started was not the problem; being consistent was! I had to be willing to make a good investment in myself for myself and for my children. A songwriter said, "Sometimes I've gotta remind myself what I've been called to do." I had to remind myself that God had called me for his own purpose and that I had a destiny; I had not yet begun to tap into the work that God had for me to do. I had to remember the word that Bishop Covington had spoken to me and to hold on to the promises of God. Meditating upon these things gave me courage, strength, and a constant hope in God no matter what. I only allowed myself a short period of time to have a pity party, and then it was time to move on.

I was very blessed that after the preacher and I had gone our separate ways, I only saw him about four times over a period of about twelve or thirteen years, and I maybe spoke with him about the same number of times as well. He had been engaged two times to two different women and had more children by others. Each of these situations helped me to realize where I was with forgiveness toward the preacher and healing from the preacher. I was so filled with anger and hurt. The thought of him moving on to what I thought was a good situation made my blood boil, so to speak. I didn't think of him as deserving of any happiness, as he had not acknowledged any wrongdoing toward me or my children. But I also had to remember that no matter what had happened to me or the children where the preacher was concerned, there was my toddler, who was also the preacher's son, who would be most affected. Sometimes we think that because children are children, that they aren't affected so much by what goes on around them. I had lived long enough to know that just the opposite is true. I knew that each of my children was clearly affected by all that happened. I was especially concerned, though, for my youngest son. I knew that I had to protect him from the danger of repeating that type of life, and from people who would judge him because of who his father was and not allow him to be his own person. I had to be careful myself to never take out any of my own frustrations out on him and to never speak negatively of his father in his presence. I knew that unless the preacher made some real life changes, it would only be a matter of time before my son would be able to see the sad truth for himself.

While I purposed not to keep in touch with his family, I always maintained that I would not keep them from seeing him if they wanted to. Unfortunately, for years no one ever tried to see him. I'm sure this was good for us, though, as I look back. It had to help me in becoming healed and being able to move forward with my life. There were many days that my children wanted to know if the preacher would be coming back; clearly he would not be coming back. They lived with a certain level of fear that the preacher would come into the house again—that he would just appear out of nowhere and and that there would be more fighting. I had to calm these worries as best I could by telling them that we would be okay and that if we needed the police, all we had to do was call. No matter what I said, only time and prayer could really make it better. We were all deeply wounded and lived with a certain level of fear as a result of all that we had been through with the preacher.

I knew that I had been freed by the mercy of God and that we both lived to tell about it. I found it to be a top priority to nurture and be more affectionate and loving, and to encourage them with words that empower or make people feel good about themselves. The preacher would say nice things sometimes, but when you are mostly negative, it takes maybe a hundred positives to kill that one negative that was spoken. In time, I trusted that each of them would be restored to a healthy place emotionally and mentally. I was mainly concerned about my daughters, because they were able to see and to know enough of what had really occurred because of their ages at the time, while my sons were at younger ages. The most important thing was that we had a chance to begin again.

As time passed, I found myself crying more and more. The reality of my life began to weigh on my emotions—the time I had wasted and the mess I had put my children through. Although the preacher was gone, I felt his presence for a long time. That was not a good thing either. With a lot of prayer and my mind-set change, it improved greatly. I found it challenging—to say the least—to keep my face when I heard his name or any part of it! I literally hated to hear his name; I remember stopping certain people before they could get it all out. It was as though his name had become profanity in my ears. Anything that reminded me of him was almost too much to deal with. I knew I had to learn to let go in order to really begin a new life. To feel this strongly was clearly evidence of my need for deliverance and forgiveness. To hold on to this meant allowing him to continue to control me and my life in his absence. The thought of that helped me to begin making that turn.

There was a special service going on at my home church, Power House of Deliverance, and some friends and I went. I remember Evangelist Iona Locke was preaching; when she preached, at a certain point I felt as though no one was there but me. She spoke right into my very soul, about being controlled, abused, and in bondage. I cried out to God and felt such a weight being lifted from me. My clothes were so wet that they stuck to me. Those that were with me knew that God was using her because they knew my story, so to speak! I knew that God was with me and that he was concerned about my family; he continued to show up for me, giving me what I needed. Thank God for every small victory!

After being separated for about a year, I met the man who is now my husband of ten years. We spent about five and a half years getting to know each other before we married. After we had been married, he was presented with dealing with some of the aftermath or residual effects of our past life of abuse. Some of my children didn't handle his constant presence well at first; they were not sure of what would happen. As for myself, I was very insecure and still had some emotional scars, though no one would ever know. I functioned as though all was well with me. Today there are still some things present with me, but they are under control. I have a very low tolerance for yelling, and I refuse to continue to be around people—family or not—that like to be controlling or manipulative. My times spent with them have to be few and far between. Today I live a peaceful life through the Lord Jesus Christ, my husband, and the family we have.

I do not wish my experiences upon anyone. However, I must say that this experience helped me to become the woman of God, the mother, and the wife that I am today! For this I tell God thank you! Because I am free today, I desire to empower others that they too may overcome abuse. While many women are abused, we must be careful to recognize that men are abused as well. I can only imagine that for them it is more difficult to speak out, to seek help, and to find a safe haven. It can easily be viewed as a weakness for men to report abuse, and it can also be embarrassing. Abuse is never okay, and it should never be accepted as such. For every person who has suffered or may be suffering domestic violence, I encourage you to seek help, whether it is intense counseling or refuge in a shelter. It is not okay for a man to hit a woman or for a woman to hit a man. May God place people in your path that you will choose to receive support from. May God strengthen you and give you hope for a better tomorrow. May his love cover you and remind you that you are made by him and for him! Psalm 139:14 says, "I will praise thee;, for I am fearfully and wonderfully made…marvelous are thy work and that my soul knoweth right well (New King James Version).

Bound to Be Free

I ask myself, where am I
But then who am I?

There I was running scared, needing the comfort of one who cared

Red flags flying high
With every rule you defy

True colors are shining through
May God have mercy on you!

Covered wounds upon my chest
While my faith in God is put to the test

Finally I'm taking a stand
For I know I'm in the Master's hand

What you did not know
And you could not see is that I was
Bound to be free, that's me

Chapter 13

Generational Curses

The Bible speaks of generational curses, or the iniquity of the fathers being visited upon the third and fourth generations of those that hate God. I remember that when I was just a very young child, my mother always had a picture of my great-grandmother, the late Daisy Bell Cornelius; the picture was always on a shelf in the living room. She died before I was born, so I never knew her. I began to ask my mother different questions about her. She told me that Grandma Daisy was a Christian woman, very nice, but that my great-grandfather, on the other hand, was not kind. She said he would be mean to my Grandma Daisy, and that he oftentimes would hit her.

My mother also shared with me how my grandparents, her parents, would oftentimes fight, and that she would have to go out on the back porch while they argued and were physical with each other. My uncle Bruce G. Malone, who was much younger than my mother, recalls them fighting, but he doesn't know who the aggressor was.

MY MOTHER BETWEEN THE AGES OF 5-7, TAKEN IN TOLEDO, OHIO ONE SUMMER.

*MY GRANDFATHER THE LATE
WALTER MALONE SENIOR "NED"*

Marva J. Edwards

HERE MY GRANDMOTHER THE LATE VIRGINIA "Muh' MALONE

My great-aunt, the late Maebelle Smoot, my grandmother's sister, fled North Carolina fearing for her life. Her husband was out to cause her bodily harm. She went to Washington, DC, and later took refuge in Toledo, Ohio. She still refused to return to North Carolina after the death of her mother. She lived in Toledo until her death in 2007

My mother, the late Barbara Malone Johnson, was involved in a couple of abusive relationships as well. There was one relationship in particular where her life could have been lost as a result of domestic violence very easily. I don't know that I've seen the type of strength and courage that she had to possess to overcome the severity of what was done to her by her abuser.

My mother's brother, Bruce Grant Malone, has struggled with domestic violence as well. Although he has not been the victim, he has been the abuser in the past. He acknowledges that this is clearly a cycle that needs to be broken, and he strives to overcome and change that type of behavior.

UNCLE BG (BRUCE GRANT MY MOTHER'S BROTHER).

(2)

if you should come home.

Darling from the bottom of my heart I want you home more than anything in this world. I have not touched another woman since you and don't intend to, and I have only drank twice. Honey I have made up my mind to be the kind of Husband you want me to be and never lay another hand on you. I will admit I have been wrong, very wrong but I would like to have another chance to make up for that.

Wayne & I went to see Tarzan yesterday at National, he had a good time, but he's always asking me when are you all coming home and all I can say is soon so you see we

This letter was written to my great-aunt Maebelle, from her husband at the time, J. Smoot, in 1959, soon after she left him.

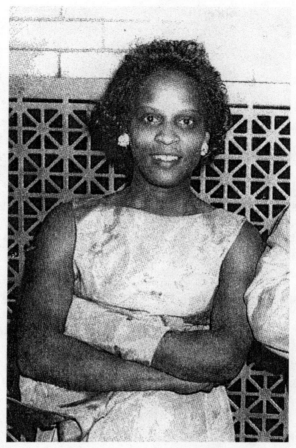

This is my aunt Maebelle. Photo taken sometime after she fled North Carolina. Photo in Toledo, Ohio.

Letter written to my great-aunt Maebelle, from her sister, Virginia C. Malone, in 1959, the year she left Greensboro, North Carolina.

By now, you have read about my experience in part as it relates to domestic violence. It was only about five years ago that it occurred to me how long domestic violence has plagued my family. We were each reared by at least one parent who was a victim and/or a survivor of domestic violence. I cannot say how or why it all began, but the cycle has to be broken. While our parents survived the danger, we were somewhat caught by the trauma of it all. We never can know completely how children are affected by domestic violence or when it will all unfold, or even how it will unfold. Because we have other experiences that are different and we mature at different rates—among other factors—we cannot truly know how and when. The truth is that the effects will manifest at some point in time. I was able to see more clearly, but not fully, how my own children have been affected by domestic violence. I came to learn so much more over the years, but particularly during the process of completing *Bound to Be Free*. Unfortunately, with those family members mentioned by name and many who are not, we have either been the victim of domestic violence or the abuser. I believe in the proverb that says, "Children learn what they live." Truly we did; that seed of abuse was sown. However, with each day we must continue to strive to overcome that stronghold in our lives and live in victory. For those of us who have overcome already, it is pertinent that you and I position ourselves to help others, that they may share in the joy of truly living and their right to be free of domestic violence. It is easy to pronounce judgment when you look from the outside in. "I believe it is important to live well enough that others desire to allow you to look from the inside out." I believe that there were things about each of my family members mentioned that have passed that we did not understand, things they said that didn't quite make sense to many of us, or even decisions they made that seemed odd. I believe it to have been in part as a result of what lessons life had taught them through their personal encounters and struggles with domestic violence. Although they may not have been able to articulate it, for whatever reason, the message rings more clearly. When I consider the little I know about their struggles with abuse, I must admire the fact that they maintained themselves and their families as well as they did; the love and the care they provided for their families is appreciated even more. The fact that though they were not fully healed themselves, they were able to love as they did exemplifies remarkable strength, courage, and great resilience!

Though I didn't know my great-grandmother personally, I know what was shared with me as it relates to her—her ability to survive her situation with the help of God and to later have enough hope and faith in God to move forward.

Because my children were exposed to domestic violence, I had to purpose to educate them continually about domestic violence—warning signs as well as what the word of God has to say concerning generational curses. While this part of my life is far from desirable, it is the reality of many men, women, and children. It is a season out of many seasons of my life that I thought needed to be shared prayerfully to the benefit of many.

To the abused, you must know that your abuser will oftentimes apologize and attempt to make peace; acknowledge wrongdoing for the moment only! You must also be aware of the fact that in the eyes of your abuser, you will never be good enough, do enough, say the right things, or do the right things to their satisfaction, but instead you will always come up short in their eyes. There will be many nights spent wondering, Why me? How did this happen to me? and or How did I let this happen to me? There will also be many nights that you will soak your pillow with your own tears because of the pain and the agony that you carry. Days of feeling incredibly low and perhaps feeling lifeless will increase. Those times of asking yourself if life is worth living will increase until you decide that enough is enough. May God give you the strength, the courage, and the will to choose to be free and to be whole!

To the abuser, you must come to a point of being true to yourself and acknowledging that you have a problem. Be willing to seek out resources to help you work through your anger and your violent behavior. Take advantage of the time that you have in this moment and get help. There is hope for you!

It is my belief that each of our lives has been affected by domestic violence in one way or another. Therefore, it is critical to the well-being of our children's children and their children and the generations to follow that we begin to educate people in the area of domestic violence and that we support efforts that provide resources for abused women and men. The numbers of victims who are being abused continue to escalate. The generation of abusers is becoming younger in age, involving more teenage girls and boys. Oftentimes there are lifelong consequences: not feeling adequate, aggressiveness, sense of entitlement, possessiveness, and being abusive as well. The list can go on and on. Unless we make a choice to fight and join the cause of fighting all manner of domestic violence, we help to stimulate our society with a group of potentially angry, aggressive repeaters of the violence done to them. Remember that while domestic violence may be a personal issue, it is also a national issue. You are not alone in your suffering. There's help available, for you are also "bound to be free".

I leave you with 1 Corinthians 13:4–5: "Love is patient and kind, never jealous or envious, never boastful or proud, never haughty or selfish or rude. Love does not demand its own way."

Chapter 14

Characteristics of Abusers

Abusers are typically controlling; they abuse verbally, seek to isolate the victim, and are often cruel. When one seeks to improve himself or herself or strives to show more independence, the abuser may become even more controlling.

They feel some sense of entitlement; they believe that they have rights to you or to what you have, but they have little to no sense of responsibility. The abuser will also try to justify the abuse/violence when they are not getting their way.

Abusers usually view their victims as their personal property, therefore being possessive. They do not see their companion as a mate.

They are very manipulative; they will portray the victim as being crazy or as having a problem while lifting themselves up to being good and right.

Abusers try to make light of the abuse and its effects, and they refuse to acknowledge it in many cases, being in denial.

The abuser almost always blames the victim for the abuse having happened. She said something, did something, or failed to say or do something. This behavior is known as *victim blaming*.

One out of every four women has suffered domestic violence. It is oftentimes heightened with the use of drugs and alcohol. Some who have been the abuser have told me that such substances alter thinking and the ability to make sound judgments. They also magnify whatever the issue is to something far greater than what's normal.

The statistics on domestic violence in North Carolina alone are alarming. If you know anyone who is being abused, please provide him or her with this number so that they might benefit from the services available to provide a safe place and protection and the hope to begin again.

National Domestic Violence Hotline 1800 799 7233 and TTY 1800 787 3224

About the Author

Marva Edwards knew all about challenges from a very young age, and what it took to overcome them. What she didn't realize though, is that life would push her to a point where the surroundings no longer resembled that which she knew. Where reason did not reside, peace did not exist, and help was not recognized. The one person that was supposedly committed to her until death do they part, was trying to kill her. Marva couldn't go to her pastor for help because he was, in fact, the man she married! She was not a weak person at all, but the fear for herself and her children zapped her strength. She knew that even though the physical pain was more than she could ever imagine enduring, she had to gather what was left long enough to save herself and her children. It was then that Marva knew that though she felt trapped, her spiritual faith would carry her, and she was Bound To Be Free" again.

Marva has served as a community worker, chaired a Community Development Corporation, performed ground work for HIV testing and has served in the Pastorate for over 10 years among other achievements in Greensboro, North Carolina. Her greatest joy is her family and her work in ministry!

Written by Roberta Boyd-Norfleet

LaVergne, TN USA
11 January 2011
211886LV00004B/3/P